FIRST EDITION

Francis Frith's
Around Folkestone

Photographic Memories

Francis Frith's
Around Folkestone

Paul Harris

FRITH
BOOK Co

Published in the United Kingdom in 2000 by
Frith Book Company Ltd

Text and Design copyright © Frith Book Company Ltd
Photographs copyright © The Francis Frith Collection

British Library Cataloguing in Publication Data

Francis Frith's Around Folkestone
Paul Harris
ISBN 1-85937-124-8

Frith Book Company Ltd
Frith's Barn, Teffont,
Salisbury, Wiltshire SP3 5QP
Tel: +44 (0) 1722 716 376
Email: info@frithbook.co.uk
www.frithbook.co.uk

Printed and bound in Great Britain

Front Cover: **The Leas 1901** 48052

Contents

Francis Frith: *Victorian Pioneer*

FRANCIS FRITH, Victorian founder of the world-famous photographic archive, was a complex and multitudinous man. A devout Quaker and a highly successful Victorian businessman, he was both philosophic by nature and pioneering in outlook.

By 1855 Francis Frith had already established a wholesale grocery business in Liverpool, and sold it for the astonishing sum of £200,000, which is the equivalent today of over £15,000,000. Now a multi-millionaire, he was able to indulge his passion for travel. As a child he had pored over travel books written by early explorers, and his fancy and imagination had been stirred by family holidays to the sublime mountain regions of Wales and Scotland. 'What a land of spirit-stirring and enriching scenes and places!' he had written. He was to return to these scenes of grandeur in later years to 'recapture the thousands of vivid and tender memories', but with a different purpose. Now in his thirties, and captivated by the new science of photography, Frith set out on a series of pioneering journeys to the Nile regions that occupied him from 1856 until 1860.

Intrigue and Adventure

He took with him on his travels a specially-designed wicker carriage that acted as both dark-room and sleeping chamber. These far-flung journeys were packed with intrigue and adventure. In his life story, written when he was sixty-three, Frith tells of being held captive by bandits, and of fighting 'an awful midnight battle to the very point of surrender with a deadly pack of hungry, wild dogs'. Sporting flowing Arab costume, Frith arrived at Akaba by camel seventy years before Lawrence, where he encountered 'desert princes and rival sheikhs, blazing with jewel-hilted swords'.

During these extraordinary adventures he was assiduously exploring the desert regions bordering the Nile and patiently recording the antiquities and peoples with his camera. He was the first photographer to venture beyond the sixth cataract. Africa was still the mysterious 'Dark Continent', and Stanley and Livingstone's historic meeting was a decade into the future. The conditions for picture taking confound belief. He laboured for hours in his wicker dark-room in the sweltering heat of the desert, while the volatile chemicals fizzed dangerously in their trays. Often he was forced to work in remote tombs and caves where conditions were cooler. Back in London he exhibited his photographs and was 'rapturously cheered' by members of the Royal Society. His reputation as a photographer was made overnight. An eminent modern historian has likened their impact on the population of the time to that on our own generation of the first photographs taken on the surface of the moon.

Venture of a Life-Time

Characteristically, Frith quickly spotted the opportunity to create a new business as a specialist publisher of photographs. He lived in an era of immense and sometimes violent change. For the poor in the early part of Victoria's reign work was a drudge and the hours long, and people had precious little free time to enjoy themselves. Most had no transport other than a cart or gig at their disposal, and had not travelled far beyond the boundaries of their own town or village. However, by the 1870s, the railways had threaded their way across the country, and Bank Holidays and half-day Saturdays had been made obligatory by Act of Parliament. All of a sudden the ordinary working man and his family were able to enjoy days out and see a little more of the world.

With characteristic business acumen, Francis Frith foresaw that these new tourists would enjoy having souvenirs to commemorate their days out. In 1860 he married Mary Ann Rosling and set out with the intention of photographing every city, town and village in Britain. For the next thirty years he travelled the country by train and by pony and trap, producing fine photographs of seaside resorts and beauty spots that were keenly bought by millions of Victorians. These prints were painstakingly pasted into family albums and pored over during the dark nights of winter, rekindling precious memories of summer excursions.

The Rise of Frith & Co

Frith's studio was soon supplying retail shops all over the country. To meet the demand he gathered about him a small team of photographers, and published the work of independent artist-photographers of the calibre of Roger Fenton and Francis Bedford. In order to gain some understanding of the scale of Frith's business one only has to look at the catalogue issued by Frith & Co in 1886: it runs to some 670 pages, listing not only many thousands of views of the British Isles but also many photographs of most European countries, and China, Japan, the USA and

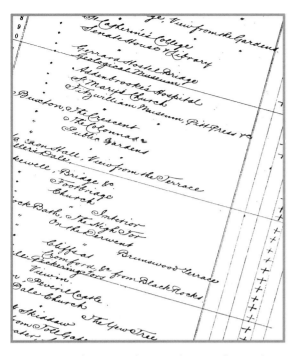

1895 a new size of postcard was permitted called the court card, but there was little room for illustration. In 1899, a year after Frith's death, a new card measuring 5.5 x 3.5 inches became the standard format, but it was not until 1902 that the divided back came into being, with address and message on one face and a full-size illustration on the other. *Frith & Co* were in the vanguard of postcard development, and Frith's sons Eustace and Cyril continued their father's monumental task, expanding the number of views offered to the public and recording more and more places in Britain, as the coasts and countryside were opened up to mass travel.

Francis Frith died in 1898 at his villa in Cannes, his great project still growing. The archive he created continued in business for another seventy years. By 1970 it contained over a third of a million pictures of 7,000 cities, towns and villages. The massive photographic record Frith has left to us stands as a living monument to a special and very remarkable man.

Canada – note the sample page shown above from the hand-written *Frith & Co* ledgers detailing pictures taken. By 1890 Frith had created the greatest specialist photographic publishing company in the world, with over 2,000 outlets – more than the combined number that Boots and W H Smith have today! The picture on the right shows the *Frith & Co* display board at Ingleton in the Yorkshire Dales. Beautifully constructed with mahogany frame and gilt inserts, it could display up to a dozen local scenes.

Postcard Bonanza

The ever-popular holiday postcard we know today took many years to develop. In 1870 the Post Office issued the first plain cards, with a pre-printed stamp on one face. In 1894 they allowed other publishers' cards to be sent through the mail with an attached adhesive halfpenny stamp. Demand grew rapidly, and in

Frith's Archive: *A Unique Legacy*

FRANCIS FRITH'S legacy to us today is of immense significance and value, for the magnificent archive of evocative photographs he created provides a unique record of change in 7,000 cities, towns and villages throughout Britain over a century and more. Frith and his fellow studio photographers revisited locations many times down the years to update their views, compiling for us an enthralling and colourful pageant of British life and character.

We tend to think of Frith's sepia views of Britain as nostalgic, for most of us use them to conjure up memories of places in our own lives with which we have family associations. It often makes us forget that to Francis Frith they were records of daily life as it was actually being lived in the cities, towns and villages of his day. The Victorian age was one of great and often bewildering change for ordinary people, and

though the pictures evoke an impression of slower times, life was as busy and hectic as it is today.

We are fortunate that Frith was a photographer of the people, dedicated to recording the minutiae of everyday life. For it is this sheer wealth of visual data, the painstaking chronicle of changes in dress, transport, street layouts, buildings, housing, engineering and landscape that captivates us so much today. His remarkable images offer us a powerful link with the past and with the lives of our ancestors.

Today's Technology

Computers have now made it possible for Frith's many thousands of images to be accessed almost instantly. In the Frith archive today, each photograph is carefully 'digitised' then stored on a CD Rom. Frith archivists can locate a single photograph amongst thousands within seconds. Views can be catalogued and sorted under a variety of categories of place and content to the immediate benefit of researchers.

Inexpensive reference prints can be created for them at the touch of a mouse button, and a wide range of books and other printed materials assembled and published for a wider, more general readership - in the next twelve months over a hundred Frith local history titles will be published! The day-to-day workings of the archive are very different from how they were in Francis Frith's time: imagine the herculean task of sorting through eleven tons of glass negatives as Frith had to do to locate a particular

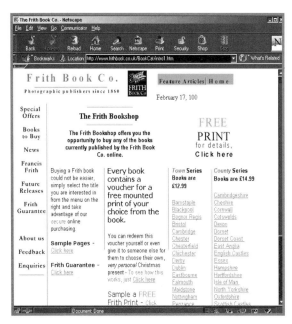

See Frith at www. frithbook.co.uk

sequence of pictures! Yet the archive still prides itself on maintaining the same high standards of excellence laid down by Francis Frith, including the painstaking cataloguing and indexing of every view.

It is curious to reflect on how the internet now allows researchers in America and elsewhere greater instant access to the archive than Frith himself ever enjoyed. Many thousands of individual views can be called up on screen within seconds on one of the Frith internet sites, enabling people living continents away to revisit the streets of their ancestral home town, or view places in Britain where they have enjoyed holidays. Many overseas researchers welcome the chance to view special theme selections, such as transport, sports, costume and ancient monuments.

We are certain that Francis Frith would have heartily approved of these modern developments in imaging techniques, for he himself was always working at the very limits of Victorian photographic technology.

The Value of the Archive Today

Because of the benefits brought by the computer, Frith's images are increasingly studied by social historians, by researchers into genealogy and ancestory, by architects, town planners, and by teachers and schoolchildren involved in local history projects.

In addition, the archive offers every one of us an opportunity to examine the places where we and our families have lived and worked down the years. Highly successful in Frith's own era, the archive is now, a century and more on, entering a new phase of popularity.

The Past in Tune with the Future

Historians consider the Francis Frith Collection to be of prime national importance. It is the only archive of its kind remaining in private ownership and has been valued at a million pounds. However, this figure is now rapidly increasing as digital technology enables more and more people around the world to enjoy its benefits.

Francis Frith's archive is now housed in an historic timber barn in the beautiful village of Teffont in Wiltshire. Its founder would not recognize the archive office as it is today. In place of the many thousands of dusty boxes containing glass plate negatives and an all-pervading odour of photographic chemicals, there are now ranks of computer screens. He would be amazed to watch his images travelling round the world at unimaginable speeds through network and internet lines.

The archive's future is both bright and exciting. Francis Frith, with his unshakeable belief in making photographs available to the greatest number of people, would undoubtedly approve of what is being done today with his lifetime's work. His photographs, depicting our shared past, are now bringing pleasure and enlightenment to millions around the world a century and more after his death.

Around Folkestone - *An Introduction*

FOLKESTONE IS OLDER than it looks. So many of its ancient buildings have been swept away by time, tide and humankind through the centuries. In the past couple of decades archaeology has found evidence of extensive settlement and farming during the New Stone Age, and the Bronze Age that followed, as a result of the Channel Tunnel construction project. Three thousand years ago, numerous small settlements that survived by farming and fishing thrived around the foot of the North Downs wherever a stream flowed. Above, on the crest of the hills, stand numerous tumuli, the graves of the chiefs of these early inhabitants of the Folkestone area.

Continental influence has never been far away, and in the century or so before Roman occupation really took hold, the Romans' influence had spread into Kent. Around the Folkestone area many Celtic coins from the 1st century AD have been found, and a large villa belonging to a British landowner once stood on the town's East Cliff. With the coming of the Romans, this building was demolished; it was replaced by two larger villas, the high quality remains of which still lie beneath the turf of the East Cliff today. There is evidence that this may have been the residence of the Admiral of the Classis Britannica, the Roman fleet that guarded the Channel from Saxon pirates. Certainly Folkestone was a place of some importance in Roman times. Not far from the villa, Roman baths and a Roman Christian church have been found in the East Cliff area, but under what name this settlement was known is debatable.

Folkestone is said to have originally been 'Folca's Stone', though no one is sure who Folca may have been. The noted local historian Dr C H Bishop expressed the opinion that the town's

name may have derived from 'Folgens stone'. Folgens was a Pre-Roman Celtic King. Where his 'stone' might be, though, is unknown. Nennius, a Welsh monk writing in the 9th century, refers to a battle between the Romano-Britons and invading Saxons at a place called Lapis Tituli (inscribed stone) on the shore of the Gallic sea. Was this Folkestone?

The Saxons, or more correctly Jutes, had settled around Folkestone by 600AD; a couple of significant cemeteries of these people have been discovered in the immediate area. Christianity become firmly established at Folkestone around the year 630 when Eanswythe, daughter of the pagan Kentish King Eadbald, founded the country's first nunnery in the grounds of her father's castle at the Bayle. Some miracles have been attributed to St Eanswythe, including making water run uphill to the nunnery to provide a clean water supply. In reality the 'miracle' was probably the result of inherited Roman engineering skills - aqueducts rather than divine intervention! Eanswythe's nunnery did not last long. Erosion and raiding Vikings put paid to it. Eventually, the establishment was restored by King Athelstan in the 10th century, but as a monastery, which later became a Benedictine Priory.

In 1213 King John made his headquarters at Folkestone for negotiations with the Pope's representatives over who would be the next Archbishop of Canterbury. John had to give up his kingdom to the Pope in principle, and accept Rome's nomination for Archbishop. In return, a planned invasion of Britain by French forces on behalf of the Pope was called off. Not much of medieval Folkestone remains; it was lost with the succeeding centuries of change.

The 18th and 19th centuries were dominated locally by the smuggling activities of Folkestone inhabitants, and by the attempts of the authorities to prevent them. Several notorious gangs were active in the area: in one incident, remembered in a ballad, Folkestone men marched on Dover gaol where some of their colleagues in crime were being held. The gaol was stormed and pulled down, and its inmates escaped into the countryside. It is said that not one of the Folkestone men was ever recaptured.

Folkestone has always been at the forefront of the defence of the realm. This role again became apparent early in the 19th century with the threat of invasion by Napoleon. Between 1805 and 1812 a chain of Martello Towers was built that stretched from Folkestone to Seaford. The Tudor Castle at Sandgate was converted into a Martello Tower, and Shorncliffe Barracks were established to the west of the town. Invasion never came, however, and for most of the next hundred years increasing prosperity transformed the town.

In 1808 construction of a proper harbour ensured the eventual start of frequent cross-

channel traffic, once the South Eastern Railway Company had purchased the finished project. In 1843 the railway arrived from London, and was quickly followed by hotels around the harbour and a steamer service to the Continent. Change continued at a dizzy pace, transforming Folkestone from a quiet seaside backwater to a top-class fashionable seaside resort. In the 1880s, the water-powered cliff lifts made their debut when both the top of the West Cliff (The Leas) and the seafront at the Lower Sandgate Road and Marine Parade were developed. Visitors could now travel comfortably between the two 'seafronts' with ease. In 1885 the Queen's Hotel opened in the town centre, followed the next year by an Art Treasure Exhibition (like a mini-Crystal Palace) at Bouverie Road West. In 1888 Victoria Pier opened, a switchback railway was built, and the Pleasure Gardens Theatre and Public Library and Museum opened their doors.

By 1900 Folkestone was the place to be; the wealthy and influential chose the town as a place to holiday or live in. The area became a magnet for the literary illuminati of the time. H G Wells had a house built; Spade House in Sandgate. Here he wrote many of his most well-known and successful novels. He also entertained a wide circle of famous authors who all lived locally, including Joseph Conrad, Ford Madox Ford, Edith Nesbit, George Bernard Shaw and many others.

In 1902 the Leas Pavilion opened as a 'superior' tea room; it later became another theatre. Bandstands sprang up along the now tastefully landscaped Leas Promenade, whilst impressive buildings rose along the wide tree-lined roads that characterised the prosperous West End of Folkestone. In 1912 no less than three cinemas opened. The future prosperity of 'fashionable Folkestone' seemed assured. Then came the First World War, and Folkestone became a front-line town. Rest camps for troops returning from action on the continent were established, and Belgian refugees arrived in large numbers; with all the military activity, the ambience of the town changed forever.

On 25 May 1917 a most tragic event occurred. A German air raid resulted in bombing across Folkestone; Tontine Street was the worst-hit area. Altogether seventy-one people were killed and ninety-six injured. Folkestone had experienced its first taste of aerial bombardment, with horrific consequences.

Between the wars, the town developed with a view to attracting a wider range of visitors rather than concentrating on the 'top end' of the market as it had formerly. The theme 'Floral Folkestone' was adopted, and flowerbeds and gardens were laid out throughout the town. A zigzag path from the Leas to the Lower Sandgate Road was built, and artificial caves and grottoes were incorporated for romantic effect. The Leas Cliff

Hall was opened - it became the area's premier entertainment venue for many years - and new gardens were laid out at an old clay pit near the Central Station. These are now known as Kingsnorth Gardens.

The East Cliff area was also developed. the newly-discovered Roman villa was opened to the public, and the cliff top above the Harbour was landscaped to create what was referred to at the time as the 'East Leas'. The East Cliff Pavilion, a tea rooms and entertainment venue, was opened in 1934. By this time the area had a small golf course, and the East Cliff Sands were developed as a bathing beach.

During the Second World War Folkestone suffered greatly. There was a mass exodus as 35,000 people left the town, which became a prohibited area. The coastline was made inaccessible by defensive works, and the town endured daily bombing, shelling and strafing, which resulted in material damage and loss of life. Folkestone's experience of World War Two is a story in itself, and has been admirably told in Roy Humphries' book 'Target Folkestone'.

The post-war period has seen immense changes, with many of the old hotels and attractions closing but new ones taking their place. The Channel Tunnel has proved a mixed blessing for the town, but substantial and ambitious improvements are now being undertaken that should undoubtedly benefit Folkestone and its residents.

I have started by concentrating on Folkestone's West End, the heart of the aristocratic resort of times past. From here I have moved eastwards through the different portions of the town covered by the photographs. Finally, I have looked at the suburbs of Sandgate and Cheriton and the countryside around.

I hope you, the reader, will enjoy this collection from Francis Frith's archives. The fine quality photographs in this book capture what Folkestone was like during its Victorian and Edwardian heyday, and how it looked during the immediate post-war period. By knowing the past we can better appreciate the present and shape the future.

The West End

The focus of the 'aristocratic' Folkestone of the late 19th and earlier centuries was the town's West End. It was here in Folkestone's heyday that the well-to-do promenaded 'to see and be seen'. The Leas had its own policemen known as 'beadles', and scruffy dress and poor behaviour were not tolerated. A man could be ejected from the Leas for not wearing a tie! The fine architecture of the West End illustrates the wealth that built and sustained this part of Folkestone. Entertainment was a genteel affair. Listening to music at one of the three bandstands or in the Leas Shelter, seeing the latest play in one of the theatres, walking the pier, or, for the more daring, riding the seaside switchback railway or taking a dip in the cold sea of the English Channel, were all popular pastimes.

Half a century and two World Wars later, Folkestone found itself in a new world where a more comprehensive mix of visitors were to be catered for. In response, the town developed its seafront along more typically seaside resort ▶

Harvey Statue 1887 19963
Folkestone's most famous son is Dr William Harvey, who first discovered the circulation of the blood in 1628. Here he is commemorated in a statue erected in 1881. The vehicle in the foreground is a bath chair, which was used in those days to transport the elderly and infirm.

lines. A boating pool and outdoor swimming pool were built. The formal gardens and seafront bandstand gave way to a roller skating rink, a funfair and amusement arcades.

In recent decades further change has occurred. A night-club, a pub, a café bar, a massive outdoor market, car parking and a new children's playground have appeared as the visiting public's needs and tastes continue to change. On the Leas many of the grand old buildings have gone, making way for new blocks of flats. Yet the best of the old is still to be found, in some cases even refurbished and improved. Hotels have been whitewashed and upgraded, the Leas Cliff Hall is undergoing development to enable it to become a major conference centre, and the Leas, now returned to its former glory, hosts thousands of visitors, particularly during the ever popular Shepway Airshow held every September since 1990.

The following pictures show the West End, the Leas, and the seafront as they were and as many can still remember them.

Clifton Road 1890 25886
At the end of the road can be seen the Pleasure Gardens Theatre, which opened in 1888. Set in sixteen acres of gardens, this complex put on not only theatrical productions but also military bands and orchestras, and provided facilities for lawn tennis, croquet and skating. The theatre closed in 1960, and was later demolished to make way for insurance offices.

Trinity Crescent 1890 25887
This lovely clear view shows a typical West End street. Traffic is not a problem here, and was presumably mostly horse-drawn, judging by the manure on the road. Holy Trinity Church can be seen at the end of the road.

Holy Trinity Church 1890 25888
This fine view of this spectacular church shows some differences in the scene from today. The church itself is unchanged, but is now surrounded by mature trees. To the right of the church is the Garden House Hotel, which we will see more closely in photograph No F35091.

The Leas 1898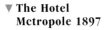
40829
The fine house seen here is now the Salisbury Hotel. In front can be seen a horse-drawn vehicle and another bath chair. It is interesting to see that some of the lawns were fenced off in those days.

▼ **The Hotel Metropole 1897**
39558
This superb building opened as the Metropole Hotel in 1897; it reflects well the opulence of late Victorian Folkestone. The hotel closed, however, in 1959, and was developed into luxury flats, though a popular Arts Centre now occupies part of the ground floor.

▲ **The Metropole Hotel 1906** 53472
The Metropole Hotel is on the left. The building on the right was the Grand Hotel. The front of the ground floor with the sunblind used to be called 'The Monkey House' locally, since passers-by would stare in to see the latest favourites of King Edward VII who sometimes used this popular sun lounge - Edward's companions were likened rather irreverently to monkeys in a zoo!

The Garden House Hotel c1960 F35091
This was a popular hotel, or at least it was until 1999 when it was gutted by fire. The building still stands, but the upper part is now an empty shell. What the future will bring is difficult to say, making this photograph an important one for posterity.

The Leas 1901 48052
This is a nice animated picture of activity on the Leas at the turn of the last century. It is interesting to look at the detail here of people going about their daily business in another age. Most of the buildings seen here have been demolished now and replaced with modern flats.

▼ View From The Leas 1906 53470

Here we see the Leas in quieter mood, with a family strolling along a cliffside path. The bandstand on the eastern end of the Leas and Victoria Pier can be seen in the background.

▼ The Leas 1912 64989

The water-powered cliff lift can be seen in this view (next to the flag). This one ran from this point just opposite the Grand and Metropole Hotels down to the Lower Sandgate Road. The lift operated from 1904 until 1940. Altogether there were four lifts linking the Leas with the seafront below.

▲ The Leas 1912 64988

In this view the lower paths running below the Leas and running down to the undercliff of the Lower Sandgate Road are visible. The Grand and Metropole Hotels can be seen, and in front of them is the West Leas bandstand. The flag near the cliff edge in front of the bandstand indicates where the lift is.

The Leas 1912 64996
We are at the eastern end of the Leas. People are enjoying the sun, reading the papers or strolling, much as they do today. This photograph affords a good view of the houses along the cliff top, which are now replaced by modern flats. The tower of the parish church of St Mary and St Eanswythe can just be seen in the distance poking above the roof tops.

The Bandstand 1912
64994
Here we see an excellent view of the East Leas bandstand surrounded by deckchairs. There is a band playing, and some people are lined up along the railings and listening whilst others stroll by. This ornate bandstand was erected in 1885, and has since been kept in a good state of repair. The deckchairs have been replaced with permanent seating and windbreaks.

The Leas 1918 68124
This photograph must have been taken just a few minutes after No 68129, as the same two ladies can be seen having now passed the cliff lift flag. The bandstand can be seen in the distance.

The Leas 1918 68129
We have gone a little further eastwards along the top of the Leas, and it is six years after photograph No 64996. Fashions have become less formal, but otherwise little seems to have changed. The flag in the distance indicates where another cliff lift is operating.

The Leas Shelter 1898
40827
This rustic-looking shelter below the Leas opened in 1894; it was a place of refuge in inclement weather, as well as a sun trap where one could relax and look over the Channel whilst reading the morning paper. Music was provided by orchestras during the winter, and by bands during the summer. Below the cliffs the Lower Sandgate Road and the seafront area can be seen.

The Leas Shelter 1912
64991
We are above the Leas Shelter some fourteen years later than the earlier view (No 40827). The skylight for the shelter is visible among the crowds, and so are the ornate ventilators. One cannot help but wonder who some of these people were - note the little boy in the sailor suit and his mother, or nanny perhaps.

◄ **The Leas Cliff Hall
1927** 80374
In 1927 the Leas Shelter
was replaced by the
much larger Leas Cliff
Hall; it continued
virtually unchanged until
1982, when extensive
renovation took place.
Further even greater
improvements were
made during 2000 to
allow the hall to compete
as a major entertainment
venue and
conference centre.

◄ **The Leas 1918** 68127
This remarkably clear picture shows the Leas Shelter, now less rustic-looking twenty years after it was built. The scene is obviously earlier than the 11 November 1918 armistice, so the war was still raging when the picture was taken. The two military men may be from one of the 'rest camps' in Folkestone, or from Shorncliffe Camp.

▼ **View from the Leas 1906** 53469
Below the Leas lay Folkestone's other main entertainment area. The two pavilions at the bottom right mark the entrance to Victoria Pier. Towards the end of the visible road, opposite the crescent of houses, can be seen formal gardens with yet another bandstand. This is a more sedate seafront than exists today!

◄ **The Zig Zag Path 1927** 80380
The wonderfully romantic zig zag path was built in 1921 as part of the 'Floral Folkestone' theme which was then being developed. The sloping path was to allow those in wheelchairs to move between the Leas and the Lower Sandgate Road.

◄ **The Zig Zag Path**
1921 71115
We are near the bottom of the path. Note the attractive ornate lamp on the left. In 2000, an amphitheatre has been completed here to allow outdoor plays and other events to take place.

The Zig Zag Path
1921 71114
We are now a little further down the path, and this picture shows the artificial caves created for dramatic effect. Little has changed here to this day, except that the tree growth has increased to give a more wooded aspect.

The Zig Zag Path
c1965 F35219
Here we see one of the artificial caves in close-up. It is no different from how it was in 1925 or 1995. The surroundings make an excellent backdrop for the theatrical Folkestone Ghost Walk that takes place several times a year.

Lower Sandgate Road, 1906 53471
This view of the scenic lower Sandgate Road shows the Toll House, which still stands unchanged to this day. Otherwise the scene has changed somewhat. The area is now well-wooded, and a superb children's playground has been constructed just where the road turns out of view.

**The Ladies' Bathing
Place 1897** 39559
At the western end of
the Lower Sandgate
Road just below where
the first toll gate was,
and where there is now
a small car park, was
this popular bathing
area. Today the bathing
tents have gone but
beach chalets line the
sea wall, against the
embankment.

▼ **The Pier 1892** 29939
Victoria Pier was opened to the public in 1888. Although it was
popular, it often had difficulty in generating sufficient revenue. The
Pavilion at the end featured various variety acts, and of course just
walking the length of the Pier was a common pastime.

▼ **Victoria Pier 1895** 35530
This is an excellent view of Victoria Pier at the height of its popularity. The notice
near the entrance advertises 'Instrumental Concerts' and 'High Class Variety'. A
notice on the Pavilion itself tells us that performances were held at 3.30pm and
8pm. Sad to say, the Pier was destroyed by fire on Whit Sunday 1945.

▲ **The Leas From
The Pier 1901** 48054
This view looks back to
shore along the Pier. The
cliff lift can be seen
towards the right of the
picture. Below the lift
track, on the beach, is a
hexagonal hut with the
words 'Camera Obscura'
on the outside. This
contained a large lens
cum periscope
arrangement that allowed
those inside to view all
that was happening
around the outside.

◄ **The Beach 1901** 48056
This is an interesting beach scene. Landward, the solid rectangular building is the lifeboat station. Folkestone had its own lifeboat until 1930. Beyond the boats, the railway carriage-like objects are Faggs Bathing Carriages. This set was for men only, and provided access to the sea as well as washbasins and towels.

**View From The Pier
1918** 68132
Here we see a very
busy beach scene
during the First World
War. A lot of people are
looking out to sea, but
what at? Was this
Regatta Day? This was
an annual event until
1946. Today, we have
the Shepway Airshow.

◄ **Marine Crescent and Gardens 1895** 35532
We are down on the seafront itself in more sedate times. The hotels beyond the gardens are still there, but the gardens and the bandstand are long gone, replaced by a bustling funfair, amusement arcades and a café bar.

View From The Leas c1965 F35212

The seafront area has changed since the earlier photographs. The last vestiges of the Marine Gardens are visible, as is the Rotunda Amusement Park and the outdoor swimming pool, all innovations of the late 1930s. Today, an outdoor market covers the former pool, and the amusement park has become a full scale funfair.

The Cliff Railway c1965 F35205

It is seventy-five years after photograph No 25885, and the cliff lift is still operating. At this time all four lifts were working. Nowadays, only two usually operate at one time. The notice at the top of the rail track says 'Fare 4d, one minute to centre of town'.

The Lift 1890 25885

These water-powered lifts were opened in 1885 and were operated by Folkestone Pier and Lift Company; they gave the tired or infirm the opportunity to travel between the Leas and the Lower Sandgate Road and seafront. They are now operated by Shepway District Council.

The War Memorial c1955 F35120
At the eastern end of the Leas, at the top of the Road of
Remembrance, stands the memorial to the dead of two World
Wars. This scene has seen much change since the fifties. Behind
the War Memorial now stands the huge block of luxury flats, 'No 1
The Leas', with an Indian restaurant on its ground floor.

The Town Centre

The history of Folkestone town centre in the 19th and early 20th centuries has been well explored in other publications. What is particularly interesting about the pictures from the Francis Frith Archives covering this area is that they convey to us the town as it was within the living memory of many, this author included. The Folkestone town centre of the 1950s and 1960s still contained much of historical interest from earlier times. The Queen's Hotel still stood proudly on the corner of Sandgate Road and Guildhall Street, a spacious Odeon cinema stood where Boots is now, and the pedestrianisation of the 1970s and 1980s was yet to come.

Despite these and other changes, the town centre shown in these photographs bears much superficial similarity to that we still see today. It is therefore particularly appropriate to present this material now, as from 2001 major town centre redevelopment is scheduled to take place. Some areas will be totally unrecognisable just a few years from now. Here, then, is Folkestone as it was in the immediate post-war decades, those in which many readers will have grown up. May these pictures bring back many fond memories.

West Terrace c1965 F35170
As we move straight on from the end of the last chapter, we see this view of the War Memorial from Sandgate Road in the town centre. The left-hand side of the road is virtually unchanged, but the right-hand side has. These fine Edwardian buildings have been demolished to make way for a MacDonald's burger bar and an Iceland supermarket.

▼ **Sandgate Road c1965** F35168

Looking up Sandgate Road from approximately the last vantage point, there is not much difference today. The Westminster Bank premises are now occupied by another bank, and obviously the cars are old-fashioned. The other difference is that the road is remarkably quiet by modern standards, even if this photograph was taken on a Sunday.

▼ **Sandgate Road c1965** F35165

This is an interesting picture. Again, the road is unnaturally quiet by today's standards. Cargills are still there, while George Stone, on the right-hand side of the road, is now a printing business with other additional offices above.

▲ **Sandgate Road c1965**
F35164
This tranquil view of Sandgate Road shows little difference to today. Most of the businesses on the right-hand side have changed, though. The timber-beamed building on the left-hand side of the road was the 'Cocker Tea Room', but i is now demolished to make way for the entrance to Sainsbury's.

◀ **Bouverie Place c1965**

F35167

We are looking toward the Bouverie Square bus station from Sandgate Road. Bobby & Co's department store is still there as Debenham's, the garage has gone and the houses beyond the buses have made way for the Saga building and a multi-storey car park. Major redevelopment is planned in 2001/02 for this site.

◄ **Sandgate Road c1965**
F35171
We are further down Sandgate Road, towards what used to be known in the 19th century as Cow Lane. The Midland Bank building is clearly shown. On the left can be seen the Odeon, a luxury cinema, now a Boots store. The impressive building at the end of the road is the Town Hall. This is now Waterstones bookshop.

◀ Sandgate Road c1965

F35169

This photograph was taken from the same vantage point as No F35167 looking east. This area is now pedestrianised, and the right-hand side now has the offices of Europa House housing the National Westminster Bank. Towards the end of the road in view on the right can be seen the Midland Bank building, now the HSBC bank.

▼ The Town Hall c1965

F35172

This is a closer view of the old Town Hall; the building is virtually unchanged today. On the left, the impressive Victorian building is the Queens Hotel. Unfortunately this was demolished in the early 1970s to make way for a nondescript office block.

◀ St Mary & St Eanswythe's Church 1892 29950

Here we see this impressive Norman church as it used to be. Little has changed, apart from the fact that the churchyard is now shaded by mature trees and no fences line the footpath. The church stands near to the site of Britain's first nunnery, which was established by St Eanswythe in AD630.

St Mary & St Eanswythe's Church 1898 40835
This is a marvellously clear view of the inside of the church as it was in 1898; it is still much the same today. A visit to this church is well recommended for the powerful medieval atmosphere alone.

Kingsnorth Gardens c1965 F35131
These beautiful gardens were created in 1928 on the site of an old clay pit as part of the 'Floral Folkestone' campaign. Little has changed in these most ornamental of gardens, although the shrubs and trees are obviously more mature now, which leads to a more wooded appearance today.

Old High Street c1955 F35028
Folkestone's Old High Street has not changed much since this picture was taken, at least in general appearance.
Most of the shops here are now trading under other names - the ironmonger, for instance, is now Copperfield's,
a gift shop. Note the old-fashioned prams.

The Harbour and East Cliff

Folkestone's prosperity really began with the coming of the railway in the 1840s, and its taking over of the harbour. Commercial possibilities were quickly realised; the huge Royal Pavilion Hotel, constructed right next to the inner harbour, became Folkestone's first major hotel development. Visitors to the town could now take day trips to Calais, Boulogne or further afield on one of the new cross-channel steamers being introduced.

During the 1920s and 30s, and again shortly after the Second World War, attempts were made to commercialise the area somewhat; refreshment kiosks, cafes and amusement arcades made their appearance around the harbour. The East Cliff was also developed at this time, with the opening of the East Cliff Pavilion as a refreshment stop and entertainment venue in 1934. Tennis courts, bowling greens, a pitch and putt and a golf course were also created on the East Cliff. The cliff top above the sands was landscaped, with seating provided on an attractive undercliff walk, now long since lost to land slipping. ▶

The Harbour 1912 65005
This interesting photograph shows sailing ships tied up in the inner harbour. In the background we can see the Royal Pavilion Hotel, which opened in 1844 hard on the heels of the coming of the railway. Next to it on the right is the County Rink, long since gone.

In the 1950s, gardens were laid out where wartime bombing had produced large rubble-strewn open spaces near the inner harbour. Meanwhile, the East Cliff sands were recognised as a potential tourist asset. The Sunny Sands Restaurant and the concrete promenade with arched changing areas, known as Coronation Parade, made their appearance.

Of course major changes have occurred since that time, particularly in the 1970s with the coming of the car ferry terminal and the Hotel Burstin. Even now, improvements are taking place to the whole harbour area, making it more aesthetically attractive. Where these have occurred, or are occurring, I will be pointing them out as we look through the photographs of this important area.

◄ **A Cockles and Whelks Stall c1965** F35154
This stall seems almost sold out. Behind the stall can be seen a little tea rooms, now much expanded and improved. The Royal Pavilion Hotel still stands in the background. It was demolished in 1973 to make way for the Hotel Burstin.

The Harbour c1965

F35213

Considerable change has occurred in the half century since photograph No 65005 was taken. Only small boats are now in evidence, and the County Rink has become a garage. The imposing building on the hilltop was the German Embassy until just before the First World War, when it was understandably closed down.

The Harbour Gardens c1965 F35153

This area, where the old High Street and Tontine Street converge, was laid out as gardens until the 1970s. Now the flowerbeds are gone - they have been replaced by tables and chairs for the nearby Royal George pub. The car park beyond now has a Tourist Information Centre, and Friday & Co Tobacconists now form the entrance to Jolsens pub.

SS 'Duchess of York' 1897 39560

By the late 19th century there was a regular steamer service across the Channel. The steamers went not only to the usual French destinations, but also, for a while, to Flushing in Holland. Cross-Channel or North Sea travel was an endurance test in those days, since the ships were not stabilised like the ferries of today.

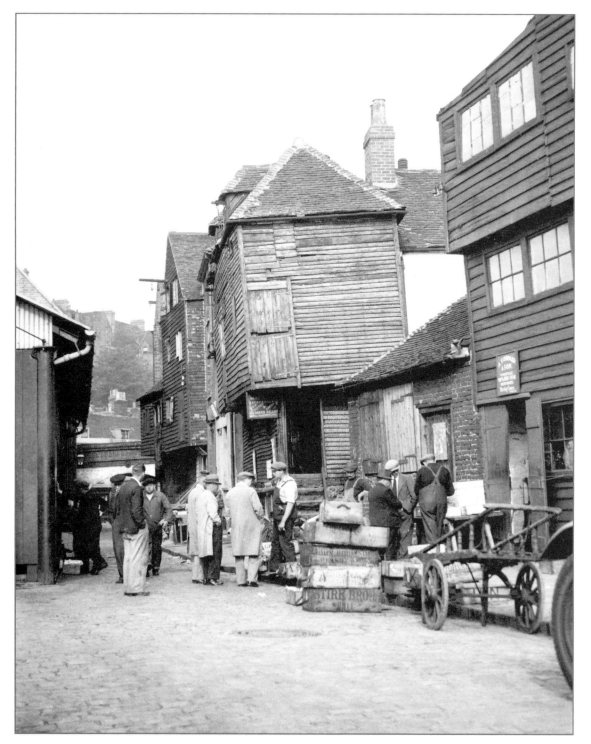

The Fish Market c1955 F35017
The market is not much changed today. Wet fish are still sold, though today the area is in a better state of repair, with motor traffic in evidence, of course. In those days, cod would have been more commonplace. Today, though, we can find many delicious alternatives on sale, such as sea bass, gurnard and pollock.

The Harbour 1906 53473
Paddle steamers are docked in the harbour. Now, the last one left is the 'Waverley', which tours the coast of Britain and calls at Folkestone several times a year. Another steamer is docked on the other side of the harbour. The well-visited Russian submarine now occupies this position.

The Harbour c1965 F35158
Again, here is a scene that has hardly changed. Today, the fishermen have a harder job landing a viable catch for a number of reasons. The cranes of the pier in the background have now gone - most freight is now transported directly onto the carrier ship by lorry.

The Harbour c1965
F35123
This photograph gives a good view across the harbour to the Royal Pavilion Hotel. To the left of the hotel the low roof of the Marine Pavilion can be seen. The popular 'Showtime' once appeared here annually, and a roller-skating rink operated. Today it is the La Parisienne night-club.

▼ The Quayside c1960 F35152

The fashions and dress sense of the early sixties are to be seen here along the otherwise unchanging quayside. The hut-like structure on the left in the distance housed an amusement arcade and toilets. The toilets are still there, but the amusements have given way to sedate seating.

▼ The Harbour 1912 65003

An attractive fishing smack sails beyond the inner harbour wall. The old town lies in the background. To the left of the boat, in the distance, an impressive church spire can be seen. This stood on Grace Hill near the library until 1975. Retirement flats now stand on the site.

▲ The East Cliff c1960

F35073

The path lined by rustic fencing below the cliff to disappeared in 1970 as a result of a landslip. The Martello Tower on the distant hilltop is now a Visitor Centre.

◀ **The Warren 1912** 65011
Here we see the impressive
undercliff before the
dramatic landslip of 1915,
which altered the look of
the cliffs nearest the
camera, and swept away the
idyllic pond that used to
attract visitors near the
Warren Halt station. The
station itself has now gone,
although there is still a halt
for railway company staff.

Sandgate

Although one of Henry VIII's castles was built here, Sandgate really developed somewhat later, between about 1770 and 1780. At this time a local shipbuilder set up business here, and had houses erected for his workers. When Shorncliffe Camp was established, the town benefited from the presence nearby of the regiments there and became increasingly prosperous.

As with Folkestone itself, Sandgate reached a peak of popularity around 1900. It was very much the place to be, and for a while became virtually the literary hub of the western world. This was due largely to the presence of the prolific author H G Wells, and the large number of famous names that came to see him in Sandgate. Amongst Wells' friends and acquaintances who visited were George Bernard Shaw, Ford Madox Ford, Henry James, Joseph Conrad and Edith Nesbit. Wells lived until 1910 at Spade House, which he had constructed by local builder William Dunk. Whilst at Sandgate, Wells wrote some of his finest novels, including 'First Men in the Moon', 'Kipps', 'Tono Bungay', and 'Ann Veronica'.

Sandgate, General View 1903 50364
This panoramic view of Sandgate from the western end of the Leas shows the Cliff Lift in operation. The house to the left of the bottom lift is Spade House, home of H G Wells at the time this picture was taken. Some remedial work is being carried out on the house by William Dunk, Builders.

Sandgate, Radnor Crescent 1913 65340
This is an attractive view of Radnor Crescent with children posing. Little has changed here, except that the pine trees are now more mature. Spade House, home of H G Wells, would be two doors back behind the photographer.

Sandgate, Upper Folkestone Road 1890 25730
Here we see the attractive houses of Upper Folkestone Road, which was renamed Sandgate Hill in 1928. How empty and quiet the road is compared to today. The weatherboarded house on the left is one of the original houses of Sandgate.

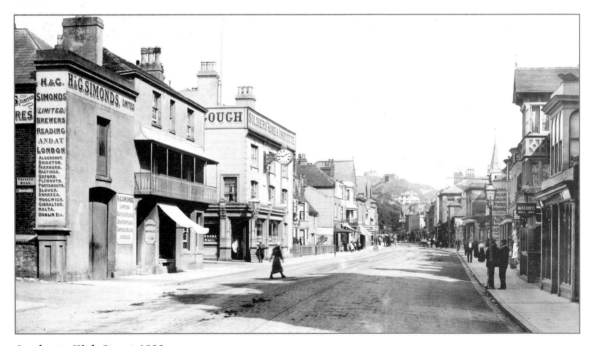

Sandgate, High Street 1899 44777
This interesting view shows some of the High Street businesses. On the right, next to the lamp, stands the Ship Inn. A little further away, on the same side of the road, is the spire of the building housing the fire station. On the hill in the distance can be seen Martello Tower No 4.

Sandgate, High Street 1903 50370
We have moved a little further west, and we have a good view of a
tram running along the tramway which can be seen in the centre of
the road. The Soldiers Home is intriguing - it is also a public
restaurant, and provides the facility of 'hot baths'.

Sandgate, High Street 1903 50369
We are looking west along the High Street.
The tramway is clearly shown in the
centre of the road. The spire belongs to
the Congregational Church, which is now
the Little Theatre.

Sandgate, Gloster Terrace 1905 56950
This interesting view shows the seafront at Gloster Terrace. A policeman talks to a man pushing a handcart on the
landward pavement. A group of children walk on the promenade, and a horse-drawn vehicle packed with people
travels toward Sandgate.

Sandgate, High Street 1906 56953
It is a busy day in the High Street, with Edwardian sartorial elegance very much in evidence. A row of vehicles lines the road on the left, whilst the horse-drawn bus to Hythe can be seen on the right. H G Wells refers to a journey by such a bus from New Romney in 'Kipps'.

**Sandgate
High Street 1906**
56952
We are a little further
west along the High
Street. Again, the
number of horse-drawn
vehicles is interesting.
A cyclist passes along
the left-hand side of the
road. On the left-hand
pavement, Bridge
Stationers and Gift
Shop can be seen.

◀ **Sandgate, High Street c1960** S55015
This view is not so different from today. The Royal Norfolk Hotel still looks much the same, and the bus stop on the opposite side of the road is still there, next to what is now the entrance to the Saga building.

◀ Sandgate, High Street c1960 S55017
Things are looking more up to date now. The ornate Edwardian lamps are still in evidence, but the horse-drawn vehicles have gone, replaced by motor cars. The old fire station with its distinctive spire had become the Public Library by the time this picture was taken. This building is now the headquarters of the Sandgate Society.

▼ Sandgate, High Street c1960 55010
Here the public library is still in its old position, but the Caffyns building on the far left has since been demolished to make way for flats. Sandgate Motors, on the right, is still a garage today.

◀ Sandgate, The Castle 1903 50371
King Henry VIII ordered the construction of Sandgate Castle in 1539, as part of a chain of such forts. In the centre is a Martello Tower, added in 1805. Since this picture was taken, the walls have been considerably eroded by the sea. The Castle is now a private dwelling.

◀ **Sandgate, The Parade 1899** 44774
Here we have another seafront picture, and more horse-drawn vehicles. The seawall here is much less sturdy than the modern defences; presumably there is now much greater danger of the sea flooding the main road.

◀ Sandgate, The Beach
1899 44776
This view shows a relaxing late Victorian scene on the beach. Note the boat up on top of the slipway. Many of the buildings in the centre of the picture have made way for modern flats during the 1970s.

▼ Sandgate, The Parade
1899 44775
Here, the sea has probably recently flooded over the seawall, judging by the shingle on the promenade. According to H G Wells, the winter of 1898 to 1899 was particularly stormy. At the time this photograph was taken, Wells lived in the cottage nearest the sea at the end of the wall.

◀ Sandgate, Sea Point
1913 65341
Here we see bathers on the beach just prior to the First World War. Note how much more built-up the sea wall here is compared to the present day. Many of these buildings have presumably been demolished. The photographer here seems to be attracting the attention of the bathers.

Sandgate, The Esplanade 1903 50367
Walkers and vehicles travel along the seafront in Edwardian
Sandgate. The shingle is again almost over the wall. Two years after
this picture was taken, the Sandgate seafront was damaged by
another severe storm.

Sandgate, Seabrook from The Stills 1899 44780
This view, from what is now known as Military Hill, shows the Sandgate to Sandling Railway with its Seabrook Station. This operated until 1931. There seems little evidence of a sea wall here, and indeed a spill-over of shingle onto the land seaward of the canal can be seen.

Sandgate, The Fountain 1899 44781
What is today the busy A259 coast road here seems almost empty of traffic. The Fountain Hotel is still a public house today, but the tea rooms opposite have long gone.

Cheriton and Beyond

Although the Manor of Cheriton dates from at least the 11th century, and St Martin's Church bears traces of Saxon work, Cheriton is in the main a fairly recently-created town. As a result of the Napoleonic scare of the early 19th century, Shorncliffe Camp was expanded and readied for possible French invasion. The large number of troops subsequently stationed at Shorncliffe led to an influx of those willing to service the needs of the camp, and hence Cheriton as we know it today came into being. The pictures in this chapter were taken before any of the modern developments affecting Cheriton and the surrounding areas took place. Particularly interesting is the Caesars Camp photograph; it was taken before the coming of the M20, considerable housing and industrial development, and the Channel Tunnel changed the scene forever.

Beyond Cheriton I have taken a brief look at the nearby villages of Newington, Frogholt, Etchinghill, Elham, Saltwood and Lympne, and the town of Hythe. Although physically ▶

Cheriton, High Street 1903 50389
Here we see a very quiet Cheriton High Street, with just the horse droppings as evidence of the occasional passing traffic! Notice the bath chairs outside the premises of the Kent Furnishing Company.

little change has occurred since these locations were photographed, each picture has a story to tell. Some locations pictured have an element of mystery about them. For instance, St Leonard's Church in Hythe contains a crypt full of skulls and thigh bones. No one is absolutely sure where all these human remains are from, or why they were all collected here. What is clear, though, is that some of the bones date back to the 12th century. Also, some skulls have remarkably Roman characteristics, according to the guide book. This seems odd, bearing in mind the age of the remains. It is an historical enigma ripe for future investigation.

Saltwood Castle, home of the late Alan Clark, former MP, Defence Minister and author of the famous Diaries, boasts several ghosts. It is also the place where the knights despatched to murder Thomas a Becket spent the night before riding off to commit their dreadful deed. The final picture of the chapter, and of the book, looks across the Roman remains of Portus Lemanis towards the mysterious realm of Romney Marsh. But that is for another day, and for a forthcoming volume dealing specifically with the Hythe and Romney Marsh areas.

Cheriton, St Martin's Church 1903 50391
Cheriton's original parish church is of considerable antiquity - it contains some stonework dating from before the Norman conquest. In the graveyard lies buried Samuel Plimsoll, who invented the Plimsoll Line. Modern housing now occupies most of the area between the church and the photographer.

▼ Cheriton, Caesar's Camp 1908 60391

The summit of this hill bears the remains of a Norman motte and bailey castle, hence its alternative name of Castle Hill. The rural scene here portrayed is now unrecognisable owing to extensive residential, industrial and highway development, and the coming of the Channel Tunnel.

▼ Frogholt, Cottages 1903 50394

We may be thankful that this beautiful cottage in the tiny hamlet of Frogholt near Newington remains unchanged today. Just a few hundred yards from here, Channel Tunnel trains whisk past on their way to and from the Continent.

▲ Newington
The Church 1903 50393
This attractive little church retains much of its charm, though its relatively large size belies the hamlet size of Newington today. The Channel Tunnel Shuttle Terminal lies just yards from the village, but is well-screened by earth works.

◀ **Etchinghill, The Stores and the Café c1960**
E157305
Etchinghill lies a few miles north of Cheriton on the way to Canterbury. Not much has altered here, though its hospital did close a few years ago. This building is still a tea rooms today.

◀ **Hythe, Beaconsfield Terrace, Marine Parade 1903** 50375
Here we see a peaceful Edwardian seafront scene. No doubt these houses belonged to the well-to-do, who were captured so well in H G Wells's novel 'Kipps' that appeared two years later in 1905. This scene remains much the same today.

◀ **Hythe, The Church
1890** 25731
St Leonard's Church in
the foreground has a
secret in its crypt:
thousands of skulls and
thigh bones are stacked
to the ceiling. Possibly
these are from an old
graveyard, but why were
they all moved to the
crypt? The claim to fame
of the churchyard is the
grave of Lionel Lukin,
inventor of the lifeboat.

▼ **Saltwood, The Castle
1890** 25896
This is the former home
of the late Alan Clark,
once a Conservative
Defence Minister and
controversial author of
'Diaries'. Saltwood Castle
is basically 13th-century,
but it was built upon the
site of much older
fortifications. The Castle
is claimed to be haunted
by several ghosts,
including that of a
Roman centurion.

◀ **Saltwood, The Rectory
1902** 48833
Across the fields from
the Castle stands this
beautiful old rectory, still
much the same to look
at today as when it was
photographed nearly
one hundred years ago.

Lympne, The Castle c1955 L335008
This beautiful private house occupies a castle whose origins stretch back to a Roman watch tower of the 4th century AD. The Castle occupies a superb position overlooking Romney Marsh; it is open to the public.

Lympne, The Marshes c1955 L335015
Below Lympne Castle, the land slopes downwards to the old course of the river Limen. The remaining blocks of masonry from the old Roman fort at Portus Lemanis can be seen on the slope. The river Limen has gradually changed course over the years, and now enters the sea as the Rother, at Rye.

Index

Frith Book Co Titles

www.frithbook.co.uk

The Frith Book Company publishes over 100 new titles each year. A selection of those currently available are listed below. For latest catalogue please contact Frith Book Co.

Town Books 96pp, 100 photos. County and Themed Books 128pp, 150 photos (unless specified). All titles hardback laminated case and jacket except those indicated pb (paperback)

Title	ISBN	Price	Title	ISBN	Price
Around Bakewell	1-85937-113-2	£12.99	Around Great Yarmouth	1-85937-085-3	£12.99
Around Barnstaple	1-85937-084-5	£12.99	Around Guildford	1-85937-117-5	£12.99
Around Bath	1-85937-097-7	£12.99	Hampshire	1-85937-064-0	£14.99
Berkshire (pb)	1-85937-191-4	£9.99	Around Harrogate	1-85937-112-4	£12.99
Around Blackpool	1-85937-049-7	£12.99	Around Horsham	1-85937-127-2	£12.99
Around Bognor Regis	1-85937-055-1	£12.99	Around Ipswich	1-85937-133-7	£12.99
Around Bournemouth	1-85937-067-5	£12.99	Ireland (pb)	1-85937-181-7	£9.99
Brighton (pb)	1-85937-192-2	£8.99	Isle of Man	1-85937-065-9	£14.99
British Life A Century Ago	1-85937-103-5	£17.99	Isle of Wight	1-85937-114-0	£14.99
Buckinghamshire (pb)	1-85937-200-7	£9.99	Kent (pb)	1-85937-189-2	£9.99
Around Cambridge	1-85937-092-6	£12.99	Around Leicester	1-85937-073-x	£12.99
Cambridgeshire	1-85937-086-1	£14.99	Leicestershire (pb)	1-85937-185-x	£9.99
Canals and Waterways	1-85937-129-9	£17.99	Around Lincoln	1-85937-111-6	£12.99
Cheshire	1-85937-045-4	£14.99	Lincolnshire	1-85937-135-3	£14.99
Around Chester	1-85937-090-x	£12.99	London (pb)	1-85937-183-3	£9.99
Around Chichester	1-85937-089-6	£12.99	Around Maidstone	1-85937-056-x	£12.99
Churches of Berkshire	1-8593/-1/0-1	£1/.99	New Forest	1-85937-128-0	£14.99
Churches of Dorset	1-85937-172-8	£17.99	Around Newark	1-85937-105-1	£12.99
Colchester (pb)	1-85937-188-4	£8.99	Around Newquay	1-85937-140-x	£12.99
Cornwall	1-85937-054-3	£14.99	North Devon Coast	1-85937-146-9	£14.99
Cumbria	1-85937-101-9	£14.99	Northumberland and Tyne & Wear		
Dartmoor	1-85937-145-0	£14.99		1-85937-072-1	£14.99
Around Derby	1-85937-046-2	£12.99	Norwich (pb)	1-85937-194-9	£8.99
Derbyshire (pb)	1-85937-196-5	£9.99	Around Nottingham	1-85937-060-8	£12.99
Devon	1-85937-052-7	£14.99	Nottinghamshire (pb)	1-85937-187-6	£9.99
Dorset	1-85937-075-6	£14.99	Around Oxford	1-85937-096-9	£12.99
Dorset Coast	1-85937-062-4	£14.99	Oxfordshire	1-85937-076-4	£14.99
Down the Severn	1-85937-118-3	£14.99	Peak District	1-85937-100-0	£14.99
Down the Thames	1-85937-121-3	£14.99	Around Penzance	1-85937-069-1	£12.99
Around Dublin	1-85937-058-6	£12.99	Around Plymouth	1-85937-119-1	£12.99
East Sussex	1-85937-130-2	£14.99	Around St Ives	1-85937-068-3	£12.99
Around Eastbourne	1-85937-061-6	£12.99	Around Scarborough	1-85937-104-3	£12.99
Edinburgh (pb)	1-85937-193-0	£8.99	Scotland (pb)	1-85937-182-5	£9.99
English Castles	1-85937-078-0	£14.99	Scottish Castles	1-85937-077-2	£14.99
Essex	1-85937-082-9	£14.99	Around Sevenoaks and Tonbridge		
Around Exeter	1-85937-126-4	£12.99		1-85937-057-8	£12.99
Exmoor	1-85937-132-9	£14.99	Around Southampton	1-85937-088-8	£12.99
Around Falmouth	1-85937-066-7	£12.99	Around Southport	1-85937-106-x	£12.99

Available from your local bookshop or from the publisher

Frith Book Co Titles (continued)

Around Shrewsbury	1-85937-110-8	£12.99		Around Torbay	1-85937-063-2	£12.99
Shropshire	1-85937-083-7	£14.99		Around Truro	1-85937-147-7	£12.99
South Devon Coast	1-85937-107-8	£14.99		Victorian & Edwardian Kent		
South Devon Living Memories					1-85937-149-3	£14.99
	1-85937-168-x	£14.99		Victorian & Edwardian Yorkshire		
Staffordshire (96pp)	1-85937-047-0	£12.99			1-85937-154-x	£14.99
				Warwickshire (pb)	1-85937-203-1	£9.99
Stone Circles & Ancient Monuments				Welsh Castles	1-85937-120-5	£14.99
	1-85937-143-4	£17.99		West Midlands	1-85937-109-4	£14.99
Around Stratford upon Avon				West Sussex	1-85937-148-5	£14.99
	1-85937-098-5	£12.99		Wiltshire	1-85937-053-5	£14.99
Sussex (pb)	1-85937-184-1	£9.99		Around Winchester	1-85937-139-6	£12.99

Frith Book Co titles available Autumn 2000

Croydon Living Memories (pb)				Weymouth (pb)	1-85937-209-0	£9.99	Sep
	1-85937-162-0	£9.99	Aug	Worcestershire	1-85937-152-3	£14.99	Sep
Glasgow (pb)	1-85937-190-6	£9.99	Aug	Yorkshire Living Memories	1-85937-166-3	£14.99	Sep
Hertfordshire (pb)	1-85937-247-3	£9.99	Aug				
North London	1-85937-206-6	£14.99	Aug	British Life A Century Ago (pb)			
Victorian & Edwardian Maritime Album					1-85937-213-9	£9.99	Oct
	1-85937-144-2	£17.99	Aug	Camberley (pb)	1-85937-222-8	£9.99	Oct
Victorian Seaside	1-85937-159-0	£17.99	Aug	Cardiff (pb)	1-85937-093-4	£9.99	Oct
				Carmarthenshire	1-85937-216-3	£14.99	Oct
Cornish Coast	1-85937-163-9	£14.99	Sep	Cornwall (pb)	1-85937-229-5	£9.99	Oct
County Durham	1-85937-123-x	£14.99	Sep	English Country Houses	1-85937-161-2	£17.99	Oct
Dorset Living Memories	1-85937-210-4	£14.99	Sep	Gloucestershire	1-85937-102-7	£14.99	Oct
Herefordshire	1-85937-174-4	£14.99	Sep	Humberside	1-85937-215-5	£14.99	Oct
Kent Living Memories	1-85937-125-6	£14.99	Sep	Manchester (pb)	1-85937-198-1	£9.99	Oct
Leeds (pb)	1-85937-202-3	£9.99	Sep	Middlesex	1-85937-158-2	£14.99	Oct
Ludlow (pb)	1-85937-176-0	£9.99	Sep	Norfolk Living Memories	1-85937-217-1	£14.99	Oct
Norfolk (pb)	1-85937-195-7	£9.99	Sep	Preston (pb)	1-85937-212-0	£9.99	Oct
Somerset	1-85937-153-1	£14.99	Sep	South Hams	1-85937-220-1	£14.99	Oct
Tees Valley & Cleveland	1-85937-211-2	£14.99	Sep	Suffolk	1-85937-221-x	£9.99	Oct
Thanet (pb)	1-85937-116-7	£9.99	Sep	Swansea (pb)	1-85937-167-1	£9.99	Oct
Tiverton (pb)	1-85937-178-7	£9.99	Sep	West Yorkshire (pb)	1-85937-201-5	£9.99	Oct
Victorian and Edwardian Sussex							
	1-85937-157-4	£14.99	Sep				

See Frith books on the internet www.frithbook.co.uk

FRITH PRODUCTS & SERVICES

Francis Frith would doubtless be pleased to know that the pioneering publishing venture he started in 1860 still continues today. A hundred and forty years later, The Francis Frith Collection continues in the same innovative tradition and is now one of the foremost publishers of vintage photographs in the world. Some of the current activities include:

Interior Decoration

Today Frith's photographs can be seen framed and as giant wall murals in thousands of pubs, restaurants, hotels, banks, retail stores and other public buildings throughout the country. In every case they enhance the unique local atmosphere of the places they depict and provide reminders of gentler days in an increasingly busy and frenetic world.

Product Promotions

Frith products are used by many major companies to promote the sales of their own products or to reinforce their own history and heritage. Frith promotions have been used by Hovis bread, Courage beers, Scots Porage Oats, Colman's mustard, Cadbury's foods, Mellow Birds coffee, Dunhill pipe tobacco, Guinness, and Bulmer's Cider.

Genealogy and Family History

As the interest in family history and roots grows world-wide, more and more people are turning to Frith's photographs of Great Britain for images of the towns, villages and streets where their ancestors lived; and, of course, photographs of the churches and chapels where their ancestors were christened, married and buried are an essential part of every genealogy tree and family album.

Frith Products

All Frith photographs are available Framed or just as Mounted Prints and Posters (size 23 x 16 inches). These may be ordered from the address below. From time to time other products - Address Books, Calendars, Table Mats, etc - are available.

The Internet

Already twenty thousand Frith photographs can be viewed and purchased on the internet. By the end of the year 2000 some 60,000 Frith photographs will be available on the internet. The number of sites is constantly expanding, each focussing on different products and services from the Collection.
The main Frith sites are listed below.
www.francisfrith.co.uk
www.frithbook.co.uk

See the complete list of Frith Books at:
www.frithbook.co.uk
This web site is regularly updated with the latest list of publications from the Frith Book Company. If you wish to buy books relating to another part of the country that your local bookshop does not stock, you may purchase on-line.

For further information, trade, or author enquiries please contact us at the address below:
The Francis Frith Collection, Frith's Barn, Teffont, Salisbury, Wiltshire, England SP3 5QP.
Tel: +44 (0)1722 716 376 Fax: +44 (0)1722 716 881 Email: uksales@francisfrith.com

See Frith books on the internet www.frithbook.co.uk

TO RECEIVE YOUR FREE MOUNTED PRINT

Mounted Print
Overall size 14 x 11 inches

Cut out this Voucher and return it with your remittance for £1.50 to cover postage and handling, to UK addresses. For overseas addresses please include £4.00 post and handling. Choose any photograph included in this book. Your SEPIA print will be A4 in size, and mounted in a cream mount with burgundy rule lines, overall size 14 x 11 inches.

Order additional Mounted Prints at HALF PRICE (only £7.49 each*)

If there are further pictures you would like to order, possibly as gifts for friends and family, purchase them at half price (no additional postage and handling required).

Have your Mounted Prints framed*

For an additional £14.95 per print you can have your chosen Mounted Print framed in an elegant polished wood and gilt moulding, overall size 16 x 13 inches (no additional postage and handling required).

---

* IMPORTANT!
These special prices are only available if ordered using the original voucher on this page (no copies permitted) and at the same time as your free Mounted Print, for delivery to the same address

---

Frith Collectors' Guild

From time to time we publish a magazine of news and stories about Frith photographs and further special offers of Frith products. If you would like 12 months FREE membership, please return this form.

Send completed forms to:
The Francis Frith Collection, Frith's Barn, Teffont, Salisbury, Wiltshire SP3 5QP

Voucher for **FREE** and Reduced Price Frith Prints

Picture no.	Page number	Qty	Mounted @ £7.49	Framed + £14.95	Total Cost
		1	**Free of charge***	£	£
			£7.49	£	£
			£7.49	£	£
			£7.49	£	£
			£7.49	£	£
			£7.49	£	£

Please allow 28 days for delivery	*** Post & handling**	**£1.50**
Book Title	**Total Order Cost**	**£**

Please do not photocopy this voucher. Only the original is valid, so please cut it out and return it to us.

I enclose a cheque / postal order for £ . . . .
made payable to 'The Francis Frith Collection'
OR please debit my Mastercard / Visa / Switch / Amex card

Number . . . .

Issue No(Switch only) . . . . .Valid from (Amex/Switch) . . . .

Expires . . . . Signature . . . .

Name Mr/Mrs/Ms . . . .

Address . . . .

. . . .

. . . .

. . . .

. . . . Postcode . . . .

Daytime Tel No . . . . Valid to 31/12/02

The Francis Frith Collectors' Guild

Please enrol me as a member for 12 months free of charge.

Name Mr/Mrs/Ms . . . .

Address . . . .

. . . .

. . . .

. . . . Postcode . . . .

Free Print - see overleaf